1001 Funny And Witty Twitter Tweets

Copyright 2014 by Charlie Bennett

Everyone appreciates a sharp wit. The most popular people on Twitter are those who offer a daily smile, or a funny joke, or a word of inspiration. Unfortunately, most of us struggle to find something funny or witty to say. Some of us struggle occasionally. Others struggle constantly.

That's what this book is all about. Now you can be witty and funny without the effort.

Tweet these daily on Twitter, and watch the followers roll in.

0001.
You can't buy happiness, but you can buy ice cream. And that's kind of the same thing.

0002.
If Plan A fails, remember that you have twenty five letters left.

0003.
Take your mom to dinner tonight. It's only fair, since you're the reason she drinks.

0004.
Things to do today: (1) Get up. (2) Be awesome. (3) Go back to bed.

0005.
You might be a redneck if you come back from the dump with more than you took.

0006.
Wouldn't it be nice if the world was flat? Then we could just push off the people we didn't like.

0007.
Sarcasm is a better option than beating the hell out of people.

0008.
Women say they love men in uniform, but when I wear my work clothes from McDonald's they won't even talk to me.

0009.
I finally found out what women really want. Security. At least that's what they yell when I try to talk to them.

0010.
Always pay the bill from your exorcist. Otherwise you'll be repossessed.

0011.
The most important thing in life is to be yourself. Unless you can be Batman. If you can be Batman, then forget what I said and be Batman.

0012.
I'm not really paranoid, but I know that all of you think I am.

0013.
I was good at math until they decided to mix the alphabet in it.

0014.
You never know what you have until you clean your house.

0015.
The reason I'm me is because Superman was already taken. I'm the next best thing.

0016.
The best way to make someone remember you is to loan them money.

0017.
The reason I'm sarcastic is because shooting people in the head is frowned upon.

0018.
There are three kinds of people in this world: those who are good at math, and those who aren't.

0019.
My dog winks at me sometimes. I always wink back, in case it's some kind of code.

0020.
Nothing ruins a good Friday like realizing it's only Tuesday.

0021.
I've learned that pleasing everyone is impossible. But pissing everybody off is a piece of cake.

0022.
Say what you mean. Mean what you say. But don't say it mean.

0023.
I love gossip. I always find out things about myself I never knew before.

0024.
When I die, I want the coroner to write down my cause of death as: "He laid down the boogie and played that funky music 'til he died."

0025.
I'm not always right, but when I am it's usually all of the time.

0026.
Lazy rule number 6: If it's not on the first page of a Google search, it doesn't exist.

0027.
I just saved a ton of money on car insurance by backing up and leaving the scene of the accident.

0028.
I just saved a ton of money on Christmas gifts by discussing politics on Facebook.

0029.
Be careful what you say to old people. They don't like being old in the first place, so it doesn't make much to piss them off.

0030.
If time is money, are ATMs time machines?

0031.
The word "phonetically" doesn't even start with an f. Stuff like that is why aliens fly right past us.

0032.
Life is like chocolate candy. Occasionally you're just gonna have to deal with a few nuts.

0033.
Every day, millions of fruits and vegetables are needlessly slaughtered by vegetarians. When is the violence going to end?

0034.
Never argue with stupid people. They will drag you down to their level and beat you with experience.

0035.
I don't want to brag or anything, but I do more dumb things before 9 a.m. than most people do all day.

0036.
My dog thinks I'm awesome. He also thinks eating poop and sniffing butts is awesome. But mostly me.

0037.
Life is short. Smile while you still have teeth.

0038.
Here's a depressing thought. Just think of how stupid the average person is. Then consider that half of them are stupider than that.

0039.
Please don't throw your cigarette butts in the urinals. It makes them soggy and hard to light.

0040.
Any day I make it to sundown without shooting anyone is a good day.

0041.
I just found a whip, a mask and handcuffs in my mom's bedroom. I can't believe it. My mom's a superhero!

0042.
I'm not totally useless. I can be used as a bad example.

0043.
Becoming a vegetarian is a huge missed steak.

0044.
Okay, if we get caught and arrested, here's the story…

0045.
It's so cold outside today, I actually saw a gangsta pull his pants up.

0046.
If you think that your dog can't count, try letting him see you put three dog biscuits into your pocket, and then only giving him two of them.

0047.
Roses are red, violets are blue. Tequila is cheaper than dinner for two.

0048.
Why haven't they invented a smoke detector that can tell the difference between a burned piece of toast and a raging inferno?

0049.
I'm not saying that you're crazy. I'm just suggesting that you're one buckle short of a straight jacket.

0050.
God gave us friends to make up for our relatives.

0051.
The reason the internet is full of cats is because dog people actually go outside.

0052.
When someone rings the door bell, why do dogs always assume it's for them?

0053.
Don't take life so seriously. It's not like you're going to get out alive.

0054.
It's a free country. Eat whatever you want. If anyone tries to lecture you about your weight, eat them too.

0055.
I'm ready to go. Just remember, if we get caught, I'm deaf and you don't speak English.

0056.
There are a lot of people who should thank their lucky stars that everything I wish for does not come true.

0057.
I don't mind going to work every day. But that eight hour wait to go home every afternoon really sucks.

0058.
I don't like making plans for the day, because then that pesky word "premeditation" starts getting thrown around the courtroom.

0059.
A quiet man is usually thinking. A quiet woman is usually mad.

0060.
Stalking is when two people go for a long romantic walk together, but only one of them knows about it.

0061.
I have NOT been stalking you! By the way, you're out of milk again.

0062.
If you could choose between world peace or a billion dollars, what color would your Lamborghini be?

0063.
Save the earth. It's the only planet with beer.

0064.
Some people just seem to have an endless supply of stupid.

0065.
If I had a dollar for every time I thought about you, I'd start thinking of you.

0066.
We all have that one creepy neighbor who never leaves his house…

0067.
Fool me once, shame on you. Fool me twice, shame on me. Fool me 6,412 times, and you're a weatherman.

0068.
Losing weight doesn't appear to be working out for me. From now on, I'm going to focus on getting taller.

0069.
The guy who invented the umbrella was originally going to call it a brella. But then he hesitated.

0070.
I've been repeating the same mistakes so often they've become traditions.

0071.
If I don't clean my house soon, somebody is going to bring in blindfolded people for a Fabreeze commercial.

0072.
Mistakes are proof that you are trying.

0073.
Men never really grow up. They just learn how to behave in public.

0074.
I work out every day. (Just kidding. I take naps)

0075.
Money means nothing to me. If you don't believe me, ask me for money. You'll get nothing.

0076.
Dear Santa, This year for Christmas I want a fat bank account and a slim body. Please don't mix up the two like you did last year.

0077.
There's no better feeling than going to bed at night and not having to set an alarm for the following morning.

0078.
Don't you hate it when you're digging a hole to hide a body and you find another body?

0079.
Let's admit it. We're only friends because no one else can stand us.

0080.
I should be ashamed of myself. I'm not. But I should be.

0081.
The ideal man doesn't smoke, doesn't drink, doesn't do drugs, doesn't swear, doesn't lose his temper, and doesn't exist.

0082.
How many of you have looked around at your circle of friends and decided that you're just two clowns short of a circus?

0083.
Whatever you do, always give a hundred percent. Unless you're giving blood. Then, maybe not.

0084.
Friends don't let friends do stupid things… alone.

0085.
I saw a man at the beach screaming, "Help, shark, help!" I thought, what a moron. That shark isn't going to help him.

0086.
Today, I will be charming and sophisticated. Or, I will trip over things and spill food on my shirt.

0087.
Doing nothing is very hard. You never know when you're finished.

0088.
If killing them with kindness doesn't work, try a baseball bat.

0089.
I'm not lazy. I'm just on energy saving mode.

0090.
There's no worse feeling than lying next to someone you love who doesn't know you love them. Or how you got into their house again.

0091.
Taylor Swift waved at a boy last week and he didn't wave back. So this week she has a new album coming out.

0092.
Some people are alive today simply because I didn't want to go to prison.

0093.
I have a lot of growing up to do. I realized that today while I was reading comic books in my tree house.

0094.
No, I didn't lose my mind. It got scared and ran away.

0095.
My Kentucky girlfriend said, "Let's just be friends." But it's okay. I've got fifteen other cousins I can choose from.

0096.
You and I are more than just friends. We're more like a really small gang.

0097.
DANGER! Mouth operates faster than brain.

0098.
I am currently unsupervised. I know, it freaks me out too. But the possibilities are endless.

0099.
Can a woman make you a millionaire? Yes! But only if you start out a billionaire.

0100.
Never cook bacon naked.

0101.
The police said they want to interview me. That's strange. I don't remember applying for a job there.

0102.
Chaos… disorder… panic… my work here is done.

0103.
feet (*noun*): a device used for finding Legos in the dark

0104:
Dear sleep, I'm sorry we broke up this morning. I want you back.

0105.
Whoever came up with the phrase, "The freaks come out at night" has obviously never been to a Walmart in the daytime.

0106.
Let's take all the normal people in the world and lock them all in a giant room. That way we won't catch it.

0107.
Always be yourself. Unless you can be a unicorn. Then be a unicorn.

0108.
I'm sorry we're breaking up. But it's not you, it's me… finally realizing that you're terrible for me.

0109.
I tried to follow my dreams. But they've all put out restraining orders on me.

0110.
Statistically, six out of seven dwarfs aren't Happy.

0111.
How do you feel when you run out of coffee? I feel depresso.

0112.
Even if the voices in my head aren't real, they still have some pretty good ideas sometimes.

0113.
I'm not saying I'm Superman. I'm just pointing out that no one has ever seen Superman and me in the same place at the same time.

0114.
I don't trust joggers. They're always the ones who find the dead bodies.

0115.
Life has no remote control. Get up and change it yourself.

0116.
At my age, I've seen it all, heard it all and done it all. I just can't remember it all.

0117.
A thief broke into my house last night. He started searching for money, so I got up and searched with him.

0118.
I'm writing a book about reverse psychology. Please don't buy it.

0119.
How to stop snoring in three easy steps: Place pillow firmly over partner's face. Hold until snoring stops. Delete this tweet.

0120.
The way to a man's heart is through his stomach. Stab in, and thrust upward.

0121.
When they discover the center of the universe, a lot of singers will be disappointed they are not it.

0122.
I'm not saying let's kill all the stupid people. I'm just saying let's take down all the warning signs and let nature take its course.

0123.
If I had a nickel for every time you got on my nerves, I'd have a sock full of nickels to hit you with.

0124.
What if cats have their own internet... and it's full of pictures of us?

0125.
Politeness has become so rare that some people have come to mistake it for flirtation.

0126.
I can't clean my room, because I get distracted by all the cool stuff I find.

0127.
I'm your quiet neighbor with the big freezer and the dark house.

0128.
How to kill all your enemies: smile.

0129.
My heart has no room for you, but my trunk definitely does.

0130.
If you need me this weekend, just call the jail.

0131.
No matter how old you are, an empty wrapping paper tube is still a light saber.

0132.
When you wait for a waiter in a restaurant, does that make you a waiter waiter?

0133.
Before you date my daughter, you should know that I am a father with a gun collection, a shovel, and a big back yard.

0134.
All you need is love. But beer doesn't hurt either.

0135.
When two egotists meet, it's an I for an I.

0136.
I started a new exercise program today, and I'm exhausted. Tomorrow I'll only do two sit ups instead of three.

0137.
When life hands you a pile of crap, say "Yippee! Fertilizer!"

0138.
My imaginary friend thinks you have serious mental problems.

0139.
I tend to offend everyone eventually. If I haven't offended you yet, please take a number and wait.

0140.
I cleaned out my back seat this morning, if anyone needs 37 half filled bottles of drinking water.

0141.
I *told* you I'd be ready in five minutes. Stop calling me every half hour.

0142.
Merry Christmas! (Sorry, I'm stuck in a time warp)

0143.
If someone breaks your heart, just punch them in the face. Seriously. Just punch them in the face and go get ice cream.

0144.
Organized people are just too lazy to look for things.

0145.
I'm really not lazy. I just enjoy doing nothing.

0146.
The main problem with the world is that the intelligent people are full of doubt, and the stupid ones are full of confidence.

0147.
Life's too short to dance with ugly men.

0148.
I put hot sauce on my hot sauce.

0149.
Some people are such treasures you really want to bury them.

0150.
Today's a special day for me. I finally got paroled for that whole mass murderer thingy.

0151.
If Mars had earthquakes, would they be called marsquakes?

0152.
When lightning strikes the ocean why don't all the fish die?

0153.
If there's a speed of light and a speed of sound, why isn't there a speed of smell?

0154.
Can crop circles be square?

0155.
Is there ever a day when mattresses *aren't* on sale?

0156.
How come lemon dishwashing liquid contains real lemon juice, but lemon juice contains artificial flavorings?

0157.
Clap if your underwear is clean.

0158.
What do you call a man with half a brain? Gifted.

0159.
I may not be perfect, but parts of me are awesome.

0160.
No trespassing at my place. Violators will be shot. Survivors will be shot again.

0161.
I can only please one person a day. Today is not your day. In fact, tomorrow doesn't look good either.

0162.
Age is not important unless you are cheese.

0163.
Exactly what part of "Go away!" don't you understand?

0164.
Vampires don't sparkle, and they're creepy. Call the cops.

0165.
I change my underwear on the first of every month, whether they're dirty or not.

0166.
If you knew what I was thinking, you'd be smiling too.

0167.
I didn't fall. The floor just needed a hug.

0168.
You're only young once. But you can be immature your whole life.

0169.
People accuse me all the time of acting the fool. But I'm not acting.

0170.
I've seen people like you before. But I had to pay admission.

0171.
Ha! My parents were wrong. It didn't make me go blind after all! Hey, who turned out the lights?

0172.
What's black and brown and looks good on a lawyer? Two dobermans.

0173.
I asked Spock. He said sparkly vampires are highly illogical.

0174.
My house is not messy. It's an obstacle course designed to keep me fit.

0175.
I miss being a kid. My only responsibilities were playing a lot and being home for dinner. And somebody else was in charge of my hair.

0176.
If life give you lemons... keep them. Because, hey, free lemons!

0177.
When I die, I'm gonna come back and haunt all you guys.

0178.
First, learn the rules. Then break them.

0179.
What do you call 10,000 lawyers at the bottom of the ocean? A good start.

0180.
When you go to Taco Bell and order a coke, and the cashier asks, "Is Pepsi alright?" ask him if Monopoly money is alright.

0181.
I may be old, but I got to see all the cool bands.

0182.
I am 99 percent angel. But ohhh, that other one percent…

0183.
I'm an indirect vegetarian. I ate the cow. The cow ate the grass.

0184.
Instead of putting "single" as a marital status, they should put "independently owned and operated."

0185.
Congress is back in session. Villages all over the country are missing their idiots.

0186.
It was me. I let the dogs out.

0187.
Right now, I could be doing a thousand different things, if this stupid computer wasn't forcing me to look at it.

0188.
Happy everything. Now leave me alone until next year.

0189.
Last words of a redneck: "Hey, y'all! Watch this!"

0190.
Don't mess with old guys. They can't fight you any more, so they'll just shoot you instead. Then they'll take a nap.

0191.
My ex girlfriend has more issues than National Geographic.

0192.
Life is like a potato.... What? I have to explain *everything* to you?

0193. To be old and wise, you first have to be young and stupid.

0194.
Dear auto correct, Stop correcting my swear words, you stupid piece of shut.

0195.
I wake up with a good attitude every day. Then idiots happen.

0196.
I just realized this morning that I'm an adult. When did that happen, and how do I make it stop?

0197.
Be nice to your children. They're the ones who will be choosing your nursing home.

0198.
It's not that I'm not a people person. It's just that I'm not a stupid people person. Hey, but please don't take it personally.

0199.
Facebook needs to add a "Who Cares?" button beside "Like."

0200.
Remember when we were young, and couldn't wait to grow up? Wow, were we stupid, or what?

0201.
We all have that one friend who's in their own little world. And if you have no such friend, then it's you.

0202.
Just because you're talking doesn't mean you're making sense.

0203.
I stopped fighting my inner demons. Now we're on the same side.

0204.
If I've offended any of you, then my efforts have been rewarded.

0205.
I'm telling you, officer. The body was already here when I arrived.

0206.
At my age, any day I get out of bed is a good day.

0207.
How do I block you in real life?

0208.
This is the 23,174th consecutive day I have not used algebra.

0209.
Marriage is life a deck of cards. You start out with two hearts and a diamond. And you end up with a club and a spade.

0210.
Sometimes I really miss my ex. But my aim is getting much better.

0211.
The man who fell into an upholstery machine has completely recovered.

0212.
The first five days after the weekend are always the hardest.

0213.
Warning: If zombies start chasing us, I'm tripping you.

0214.
Don't take life so seriously. It isn't permanent.

0215.
I'm too sexy for my shirt.

0216.
I swear, because sometimes "gosh darn" and "meanie head" just don't cut it.

0217.
Dear Math: Stop asking us to find your X. She's gone and she's not coming back. And don't ask Y either.

0218.
Slut *(noun)*: A woman with the morals of a man.

0219.
Part of a best friend's job is to immediately clear your computer's history if you die.

0220.
Nothing sucks more than that moment during an argument when you realize that you're wrong.

0221.
I totally take back all those times I didn't want to take a nap when I was a kid.

0222.
We really need a special font for sarcasm.

0223.
Was learning cursive really necessary?

0224.
Google Maps needs to start their directions on Page 4. I already know how to get out of my own neighborhood.

0225.
Bad decisions make great stories.

0226.
I keep some people's phone numbers in my phone just so I know not to answer when they call.

0227.
I disagree with Kay Jewelers. I think more kisses begin with tequila.

0228.
How many times is it appropriate to say, "what?" to an overseas customer service representative before you ask to speak to someone you can understand?

0229.
Shirts and underwear get dirty. Jeans never get dirty. You can wear those suckers forever.

0230.
Sometimes I'll look at my watch three or four times and still not know what time it is.

0231.
Never get jealous when you see your ex with someone else. After all, your parents taught you to share your old worn out things with the less fortunate.

0232.
What's this thing called "normal?" Is it contagious? Get it away from me. I don't want to catch your "normal!"

0233.
You go ahead and give peace a chance. I'll cover you in case it doesn't work out.

0234.
People who think they know everything really annoy those of us who do.

0235.
If we can't tax the rich, can we at least eat them?

0236.
We're all mature until somebody pulls out bubble wrap.

0237.
People say that I'm crazy, cheap and easy. But they're wrong. I'm not cheap.

0238.
People like you are the reason why people like me need medication.

0239.
Let's eat Grandma! No, wait… Let's eat, Grandma! Correct punctuation saves lives.

0240.
I'll never tell her this, but when my girlfriend gives me the silent treatment, it's not really much of a punishment.

0241.
There's a good chance you don't like me. But there's an even better chance I don't care.

0242.
We'll be best friends forever. Because we're both too damn lazy to find new best friends.

0243.
When one door closes and another one opens, you need to move the heck out of your house because it's clearly haunted

0244.
If crazy people could fly, my family would be the Air Force.

0245.
They say that what doesn't kill you makes you stronger. At this point, I should be able to bench press a Buick.

0246.
I'm not totally useless. I can be used as a bad example.

0247.
Synonym *(noun)*: A word used in place of the one you can't spell.

0248.
My soul was removed to make room for all this sarcasm.

0249.
Here's why I can't spell. To be this witty and good looking, and be a good speller on top of that just wouldn't be fair for everyone else.

0250.
Sometimes I really miss my ex. But most days I just smile and enjoy the thought that she's somebody else's problem now.

0251.
If I have offended any of you... good.

0252.
Of course I talk to myself. Sometimes I need expert advice.

0253.
If you have to ask if it's too early to drink wine, then you're an amateur and we can't hang out together anymore.

0254.
I took a pain pill. So why are you still here?

0255.
You know that tingly feeling you get when you first fall in love? That's common sense leaving your body.

0256.
I want one of those jobs where people ask me, "Do you actually get paid for doing this?"

0257.
You can't always control who walks into your life. But you can control which window you throw them out of.

0258.
Don't be so open minded that your brains fall out.

0259.
Sometimes giving someone a second chance is like giving them another bullet because they missed you the first time.

0260.
I changed my car horn to the sound of gunshots. Cars get out of my way much faster now.

0261.
When you really want to slap someone, go ahead and do it and say "mosquito."

0262.
Dear LOL, thanks for being there when I have nothing else to say.

0263.
Dear Optimist and Pessimist, While you were arguing about the glass of water, I drank it. Sincerely, Opportunist

0264.
You people are insane. I know, because I can recognize my own kind.

0265.
Dear radio stations, You do realize there are more than five songs in the world, right?

0266.
Sign at ski resort: CAUTION. TREES DON'T MOVE.

0267.
I had a mind once, but I kept giving people a piece of it. Now it's all gone.

0268.
I heard that internet addiction is now an officially recognized mental disorder and you can go to rehab for it. I'm only going if they have wi-fi.

0269.
Wrong is wrong, even if everyone is doing it. Right is right, even if you're doing it all by yourself.

0270.
The only thing worse than the one who got away is the one who won't go away.

0271.
Caution: I am temperamental. Half temper, half mental.

0272.
The difference between genius and stupidity is that genius has its limits.

0273.
You laugh, I laugh. You cry, I cry. You jump off a really high cliff, I yell "do a flip!"

0274.
Getting into an argument with a woman is just like being arrested. Anything you say can and will be used against you.

0275.
Marriage is a relationship in which one person is always right. And the other person is a husband.

0276.
Honestly, I'm an angel. The horns are there just to keep my halo from falling off.

0277.
I asked my girlfriend for a newspaper. She said, "Don't be silly. Just use my i-Pad." Boy, that spider never knew what hit him.

0278.
Have you ever looked at somebody and thought to yourself… "Yep. He has a person locked in a basement somewhere."

0279.
All those who believe in telekinesis, raise my hand.

0280.
Today I broke my personal record for most consecutive days lived.

0281.
If I have learned anything since joining Facebook, it's that I'm not nearly as messed up as I thought I was.

0282.
New rule: If you have lifted your feet so that someone could vacuum beneath them, you have, in fact, helped with the cleaning.

0283.
Please don't make me angry. I'm running out of places to hide the bodies.

0284.
One mind reader to another: You're fine. How am I?

0285.
A positive attitude may not solve all your problems, but it will annoy enough people to make it worth your while.

0286.
I've learned so much from my mistakes, I'm thinking of making a few more.

0287.
We had to get rid of the kids. The cat was allergic.

0288.
You know it's going to be a long day when you yell, "Seriously?" at your alarm clock.

0289.
How can I trust you when you keep running away every time I untie you?

0290. Light travels faster than the speed of sound. That's why a lot of people appear to be bright until they speak.

0291.
A cop pulled me over and said, "papers." So I said, "scissors, I win." and drove off.

0292.
Don't worry. I won't tell your secret to anyone. And if I do, I'll tell them not to tell anyone.

0293.
If you find it necessary to judge me on my past, don't be surprised when I put you there.

0294.
I've been putting a lot of thought into it lately, and I don't think this whole "being an adult" thing is going to work for me.

0295.
If you haven't grown up by age 50, you don't have to.

0296.
If you can smile when things go wrong, you obviously have someone in mind to blame.

0297.
Don't you type at me in that tone of voice.

0298.
Life is hard. It's much harder if you're stupid. But then, I guess you already knew that.

0299.
When I want your opinion, I'll remove the gag.

0300. Never laugh at your wife's choices. You're one of them.

0301.
Women always worry about the things that men forget. Men always worry about the things that women remember.

0302.
Teacher to parents: "I wouldn't worry about his grades. I'm sure you were just as stupid at his age."

0303.
Whatever doesn't kill me… had better start running.

0304.
I'm gonna start a band called "Free Beer," so that when people see a sign that says, "Free Beer tomorrow night at 7," everybody will be there.

0305.
Today has been cancelled. Go back to bed.

0306.
It's okay if you disagree with me. I can't force you to be right.

0307.
It's scary that before Facebook, all this stuff just stayed in people's heads.

0308. Yesterday a friend told me I was delusional. I was so upset I almost fell off my unicorn.

0309.
I put a Dallas Cowboys sticker on my broken vacuum cleaner. Now it sucks again.

0310.
If Plan A fails, remember that you have 25 more letters left.

0311.
I replaced my car horn with gunshot sounds. People get out of my way much faster now.

0312.
On the internet you can be anything you want to be. It's odd that so many people want to be stupid.

0313.
If you put a crouton on your sundae instead of a cherry, it counts as a salad.

0314.
It's too bad I can only delete you on Facebook and not in real life. Apparently that's illegal.

0315.
You can tell a lot about a woman by her hands. For instance, if they're placed tightly around your throat, she's probably a little upset.

0316.
Uh, oh. It looks like I picked a bad day to stop thinking.

0317.
I'm not lazy. I just don't do stuff.

0318.
You mean so much to be that if we were ever on a sinking ship and there was only one life preserver left, I'd miss you and think about you often.

0319.
frustration *(state of mind):* When you feel the need to knock the stupid out of someone but you can't because you'd go to jail.

0320.
My ultimate dream is to cut all ties with civilization, but still be on the internet.

0321.
Why is SpongeBob the main character, if Patrick is the star?

0322.
While you were busy judging others, you left your closet door open and the skeletons fell out.

0323.
Google must be a woman, because it knows *everything*.

0324.
Fight apathy. Or don't.

0325.
If you don't want anyone to find out, just don't do it.

0326.
I enjoy long romantic walks. In the middle of the night. To the fridge.

0327.
If there was a way to read a woman's mind, I'm not sure I'd want to. I mean, I hate shoes and shopping. And I already know I'm annoying.

0328.
The nice part about living in a small town is that if you don't know what you're doing, somebody else knows.

0329.
Illegal immigration isn't a new problem. Native Americans used to call it "white people."

0330.
I'm so sorry. Did the middle of my sentence interrupt the beginning of yours?

0331.
You call it lazy, but I prefer to call it selective participation.

0332.
Congressmen should wear uniforms like NASCAR drivers so we can identify their corporate sponsors.

0333.
I ate four boxes of thin mints. But I don't feel thin at all.

0334.
Don't text me in the middle of texting you. Now I have to change my text.

0335.
If dogs could speak, I'm pretty sure their favorite phrase would be, "Are you gonna finish that?"

0336.
You'd be in good shape if your body ran as fast as your mouth.

0337.
Why does Snoop Dogg need an umbrella?   Fo' drizzle.

0338.
I eat cake because every day it's somebody's birthday somewhere.

0339.
Yes, yes, I'm listening. I'm just resting my eyes. Please continue your very interesting story about whatever it was.

0340.
I hate it when I'm singing along with a song and the singer gets the words wrong.

0341.
People said to follow your dreams, so I went back to bed.

0342.
Don't judge me because I'm quiet. No one plans a murder out loud.

0343.
Scientists have discovered why female spiders eat their mates. It turns out the male spiders deserve it.

0344.
democracy: *(noun):* The freedom to elect our own dictators

0345.
The floggings will continue until morale improves.

0346.
Some people get confused when a sentence doesn't end as they salad.

0347.
Even duct tape can't fix stupid. But it can muffle the screams while you fix it yourself.

0348.
Caution: Drinking alcoholic beverages before pregnancy can cause pregnancy.

0349.
I'm only responsible for what I say, not for how much you understand.

0350.
Today's menu: Eat it or starve.

0351.
I never make the same mistake twice. I always make it five or six times, just to be sure.

0352.
We'll always be best friends, because you know too much.

0353.
I don't exactly hate you, but if you were on fire and I had water, I'd drink it.

0354.
Me: I'm going to bed. Internet: Ha ha ha. No.

0355.
A person's palm can say a lot about a person. Especially when it hits you upside the head.

0356.
Remember, you can pick your friends. And you can pick your nose. But you can't pick your friends' noses.

0357.
I'm not always right. But I'm never wrong.

0358.
Spider Web *(noun)*: A thing you walk into that instantly turns you into a karate master.

0359.
If you think education is expensive, try ignorance.

0360.
I'm jealous of my parents. I'll never have a kid as cool as theirs.

0361.
immature *(adj.)*: A word boring people use to describe fun people.

0362.
There is no such thing as automatic doors. Just gentleman ninjas.

0363.
Judging by the frying pan that just flew over my head, I did something wrong. I can't wait to find out what it was.

0364.
reality *(noun):* The annoying time between sleep and the internet.

0365.
Somebody asked me if I hugged my mom today. I said, "No. But I hugged yours."

0366.
An apple a day will keep anyone away if you throw it hard enough.

0367.
If I call you darling, will you make me pancakes?

0368.
Never get into an argument with someone who types faster than you.

0369.
People will judge you by your actions, not your intentions. You may have a heart of gold, but so does a boiled egg.

0370.
Procrastinators unite!   Tomorrow.

0371.
I would like to apologize to anyone I have *not* offended. Please be patient. I'll get to you shortly.

0372.
Dogs are great. They still love you, even though they know you're made of meat.

0373.
Statistically, 147 percent of people exaggerate.

0374.
Someone told me I tend to say random things, but I don't know what he's talking about. Spaghetti.

0375.
If vegetarians love animals so much, why do they eat their food?

0376.
Politicians should all be limited to two terms: One in office and one in prison.

0377.
Borrow money from pessimists. They never expect to get it back.

0378.
I got up this morning and ran around the block four times. I was so exhausted, I picked up the block and put it back in the toy box.

0379.
Next time you're alone with a stranger, and they talk to you, give them a shocked look and whisper, "You can see me?"

0380.
The next time you get a call from a blocked or private number, answer the phone and whisper, "It's done, but there's blood *everywhere!* Then hang up.

0381.
I'd be unstoppable if it weren't for physics and law enforcement.

0382.
You can't always control everything. Your hair was put on your head to remind you of that.

0383.
On the internet you can be anything you want to be. I choose to be Superman.

0384.
I know the voices aren't real, but they have some really great ideas.

0385.
I used to have super powers until the psychiatrists took them away.

0386.
I'm sorry. Sarcasm falls out of my mouth, just like stupid falls out of yours.

0387.
Don't raise your voice. Improve your argument.

0388.
Birthdays then: "Wow! Look at all these presents!"
Birthdays now: "Wow! Look at all these notifications!"

0389.
When karma comes back to kick you in the face, I want to be there. Just in case it needs backup.

0390.
People say you can't live without love. Personally, I think oxygen is a little more important.

0391.
I finally got my head together. Now my body is falling apart.

0392.
I used to jog five miles a day. Then I found a shortcut.

0393.
Men have feelings too, you know. For example, sometimes we feel hungry

0394.
My laundry schedule- Sort: Today. Wash: Tomorrow. Iron: Yeah, right.

0395.
If you're not willing to laugh at yourself, somebody else will do it for you.

0396.
Being honest may not get you a lot of friends. But it'll get you the right ones.

0397.
I'm not evil. I'm good… with a twist.

0398.
I love asking kids what they want to be when they grow up, because I'm still looking for ideas

0399.
I say "ouch" before I'm even sure it hurts. Just in case.

0400.
I'm confused. Oh, wait. Maybe I'm not.

0401.
People say I have a short attention spa... Hey look, a bird!

0402.
I'm so broke my nervous breakdown is on layaway.

0403.
I cook using the four food groups: canned, boxed, bagged and frozen.

0404.
Some of us learn from other people's mistakes. The rest of us have to be the other people.

0405.
My internet went down yesterday. I think my neighbor forgot to pay his bill. How irresponsible.

0406.
Whoever said nothing is impossible has obviously never tried to staple water to a tree.

0407.
Will Rogers never met Justin Bieber.

0408.
Today I am confident. I feel like Superman. I can leap off tall buildings. But only once.

0409.
Silence is golden, unless you have a toddler. In that case, silence is very troublesome indeed.

0410.
Most people want perfect relationships. I just want a hamburger that looks like the one in the commercials.

0411.
I swear it wasn't me. Unless it was a good thing. Then I confess.

0412.
Argument rule number one: If you start correcting their grammar, you're losing.

0413.
Go ahead and judge me. Just make sure you don't make any mistakes for the rest of your life.

0414.
I tried being normal once. It was the worst five minutes of my life.

0415.
I'm the quiet neighbor with the big freezer.

0416.
My death will probably be caused by me being sarcastic to the wrong person.

0417.
Respect old people. They graduated from high school without either Google or Wikipedia.

0418.
It took me a long time to lose my mind. What made you think I'd want a piece of yours?

0419.
The problem with closed-minded people is that their mouths are always open.

0420.
Tomorrow *(noun)*: The best time to do everything you were going to do today.

0421.
If you're feeling down, I can feel you up.

0422.
Either you love bacon, or you're wrong.

0423.
I once won an argument with a woman… in this dream I had.

0424.
Just because you make your voice louder doesn't mean you're any more right.

0425.
Whew! I just got a bill in the mail that said, "Final notice!" I'm glad that's over.

0426.
I'm smiling today. That should terrify you.

0427.
I just joined a group called Exaggerators Anonymous. We're a trillion strong and growing.

0428.
Therapy helps. But hitting you over the head with a shovel is much cheaper.

0429.
I don't always say something stupid… But when I do, I keep talking and making it worse.

0430.
I have bypassed crazy, skipped past insane, and gone straight to psycho.

0431.
We all have that one friend we always greet with an insult.

0432.
If someone calls you lazy, don't respond.

0433.
It's your life. Eat what you want. And if anybody tries to stop you, eat them too.

0434.
I'm running out of people I can stand this week.

0435.
Who wants to put on bear costumes and terrorize the people camping at Best Buy on black Friday?

0436.
There's nothing scarier than when you almost slip in the shower and think, "Oh, God, they're going to find me naked."

0437.
When I'm right, no one remembers. When I'm wrong, no one forgets.

0438.
You know you're broke when your baloney doesn't have a first name.

0439.
The best feeling in the world is going to bed at night and knowing you don't have to set your alarm for the next day.

0440.
The reason the internet is full of cat pictures is because dog people actually have lives.

0441.
How come know-it-alls don't know how annoying they are?

0442.
And then Satan said, "Put the alphabet in math…"

0443.
I have no need for Google. I have a wife who knows it all.

0444.
My drinking is completely under control. It's my drunken behavior that I need to work on.

0445.
I usually laugh at my own texts before I send them because I rarely say anything that's not hilarious.

0446.
It's a scientific fact. Never tell a woman she's crazy unless you want to see crazy.

0447.
When I was young, I thought I knew everything. Now that I'm old, I really do.

0448.
Haters gonna hate. Potatoes gonna potate.

0449.
Marriage is an act that allows you to annoy just one special person for the rest of your life.

0450.
I'm really not lazy. I just need lots of sleep to maintain my super powers.

0451.
We learn from our mistakes. That's why I make as many as I can. Soon, I'll be a genius.

0452.
Crazy people don't know they're crazy. Isn't that crazy?

0453.
We are best friends. If you ever fall, I will pick you up. After I stop laughing.

0454.
Sometimes you have to burn a few bridges to keep the crazies from following you.

0455.
If history repeats itself, I am so getting a dinosaur.

0456.
I did not escape. They gave me a day pass.

0457.
Just so you know, if you ever need a plant killed, I'm the person for the job.

0458.
Just because I'm awake doesn't mean I'm ready to do things.

0459.
You call it stalking. I prefer to call it intense research.

0460.
I shot my first turkey yesterday. Scared everyone in the frozen food section. I'm not allowed in Safeway anymore.

0461.
No woman ever shot a man while he was doing the dishes.

0462.
I've seen people like you before. But I had to pay admission.

0463.
So many idiots, so few bullets…

0464.
Never wake a sleeping woman. Because then she'll be awake.

0465.
I'm too sexy for my shirt.

0466.
People change. Now I'm a parking meter. Tomorrow I'll be a Volkswagen.

0467.
If someone calls you a crazy freak, tell them thank you. Nothing scares people more than a crazy freak who's proud of being a crazy freak.

0468.
Don't piss me off. I'll give your number to all the kids at the elementary school and tell them it's Santa's hotline.

0469.
Being normal? Yuck! I can't imagine how horrible that would be.

0470.
I'm not insulting you. I'm describing you.

0471.
Well, I'm here. What are your next two wishes?

0472.
Didn't do it. Wasn't even there.

0473.
I stopped fighting my inner demons. We're on the same side now.

0474.
People who think they know everything really annoy those of us who do.

0475.
Life is like a potato… What? I have to explain *everything* to you?

0476.
I dare someone to kidnap me. As soon as my medication wears off, they'll pay me to leave.

0477.
Halloween is the best day of the year to leave a dead body propped up in a rocking chair on your front porch.

0478.
Hey, I found your nose. It was in my business.

0479.
Hello spider… nice spider… let me pet you… WITH MY FOOT!... good spider. dead spider.

0480.
Tonight's menu: take it or leave it.

0481.
When your ex says, "You'll never find anyone like me again," say: "That's kinda the point."

0482.
Old people always poke me at weddings and say, "You're next." So now I started doing the same thing to them at funerals.

0483.
If I can make you smile, I've accomplished my mission. If I can make you laugh until you pee your pants, even better.

0484.
You're only young once. But you can be immature for the rest of your life.

0485.
At my age, any day I get out of bed is a good day.

0486.
I had a really bad day. First, my ex got run over by a bus. Then, I got fired from my job as a bus driver.

0487.
You don't stop laughing because you grow old. You grow old because you stop laughing.

0488.
Honesty may be the best policy, but insanity is the best defense.

0489.
If you can't beat 'em, annoy 'em.

0490.
Just because you're paranoid doesn't mean they're not coming to get you.

0491.
You inspire my inner serial killer.

0492.
Thanks for the advice. But what I really need are my own minions.

0493.
The one thing you should never be left alone with is your own thoughts. They'll eat you alive until the next morning.

0494.
Good morning. I see the assassins have failed.

0495.
I'm not smiling because I'm happy. I'm happy because I'm strangling you in my head.

0496.
My silence doesn't mean I agree with you. It just means that your level of stupidity has rendered me speechless.

0497.
Common sense is a flower that doesn't grow in everyone's garden.

0498.
If people could read my mind, I'd get punched in the face a lot.

0499.
"Sir, we're surrounded."   "Good! We can attack from any direction."

0500.
My financial advisor told me to invest in tennis balls. He said they have a high rate of return.

0501.
If I had to live without you, I'd shoot myself. But only in the foot. I love you, but I'm not an idiot.

0502.
I wonder if Chinese tourists get mad when they buy a souvenir in the United States and it says it was made in China.

0503.
Don't break anyone's heart. They only have one. Break their bones instead. They have 206 of them.

0504.
Those who say "there is no such thing as a stupid question" has obviously never worked in customer service.

0505.
I before E except after C… except when you run a feisty heist on a weird beige foreign neighbor.

0506.
Does it count as saving someone's life if you refrained from murdering them?

0507.
I hit a car this morning that was driven by a dwarf. He came over and said, "I'm not happy!" So I said, "Well, which one are you?"

0508.
Being married is having the freedom to do whatever your wife tells you to.

0509.
Never trust a smiling cat.

0510.
I wake up every day planning to be productive and then a voice in my head says, "Ha ha, good one!" And then we laugh and laugh and take a nap.

0511.
I just rolled my eyes so hard I saw my brain.

0512.
When life hands you lemons, squirt them in people's eyes.

0513.
Well, another day has passed and I still haven't used algebra.

0514.
I have decided that I no longer want to be an adult. If anyone needs me, I will be under my bed coloring.

0515.
Had the time of my life last night. Um... anybody got any spare money for my bail?

0516.
I don't know how people get eaten by sharks. I mean, how can they not hear the music?

0517.
Two blondes were driving to Disneyland. The sign said, "Disneyland Left." So they turned around and went home.

0518.
I hope I never go to jail because I haven't memorized a phone number since 2005.

0519.
I hate it when I'm singing along with a song and the singer gets the words wrong.

0520.
Having a job interferes with my plans for world domination.

0521.
Grandchildren are the reward you get for not strangling your children.

0522.
Googling your symptoms when you don't feel well is the best way to convince yourself you're dying.

0523.
Thanks for texting me first, and then ignoring my reply.

0524.
Yesterday my neighbor called the cops because I was playing classic rock too loud. The cops arrested him.

0525.
Those who jump off a bridge in Paris are in Seine.

0526.
A man's home is his castle, in a manor of speaking.

0527.
Practice safe eating. Always use condiments.

0528.
A chicken crossing the road is poultry in motion.

0529.
A lot of money is tainted. Taint yours and taint mine.

0530.
I'd like to think I'll die a heroic death, but it's more likely I'll trip over my own two feet and fall down a flight of stairs.

0531.
When someone asks, "Where's your Christmas spirit?" is it wrong to point to my liquor cabinet?

0532.
You know what's the best part of waking up early? Absolutely nothing.

0533.
From a procrastination standpoint, today has been highly successful.

0534.
I was planning to get on down with my bad self today, but then I remembered I have laundry to do.

0535.
It's not a real family get together until somebody has a meltdown.

0536.
I never run with scissors.   Whoa, those last two words were totally unnecessary.

0537.
Anyone who says I never exercise has never seen me put on a pair of jeans fresh out of the dryer.

0538.
Ladies, if you want to strike fear in the heart of your man, just look him in the eye and ask, "Notice anything different?"

0539.
I hate it when I'm all set on running a yellow light and the person in front of me chickens out.

0540.
When I was a baby an evil witch cursed me with expensive tastes and no money.

0541.
My dream job is not needing one.

0542.
My brain has too many tabs open.

0543.
Parenting becomes much harder when you can no longer say, "I'm calling Santa!"

0544.
A friend asked me the other day if I've ever paid for sex. I said I have six children. I have paid dearly for sex.

0545.
A policeman came to my house and asked where I was between seven and eight. I said, "Second grade."

0546.
Just like everyone else, I put my straight jacket on one buckle at a time.

0547.
After all those years in school, I finally know what a semi colon is used for... to make winky faces.

0548.
The best place to hide a dead body is on page 2 of a Google search.

0549.
Don't mind me. I'm just here to establish an alibi.

0550.
Sometimes I wrestle with my inner demons. And other times we just snuggle.

0551.
Instead of calling it the "john," I'm going to start calling my bathroom the "jim." That way I can say I go to the jim every morning.

0552.
When comforting a grammar nazi, I always hold them close and say, "There, they're, their…"

0553.
Everyone has the right to be stupid. But you're abusing the privilege.

0554.
You really don't have to out crazy everybody else. It's not a competition.

0555.
You cannot expect to be old and wise if you were never young and stupid.

0556.
I've been single for awhile now, and it feels great. I am stronger and more independent and free. I really think I'm the one.

0557.
Dear mind, please stop thinking so much late at night. I need some sleep.

0558.
If tomatoes are a fruit, is ketchup a smoothie?

0559.
Am I the only one who gets road rage from pushing a shopping cart through Walmart?

0560.
I'm actually a very nice person. I just don't like other people.

0561.
Shortest horror story ever: Monday.

0562.
My family is temperamental. Half temper, half mental.

0563.
A woman's mind is cleaner than a man's, because she changes it more often.

0564.
I'm very hygienic. I brush my tooth once a month whether it needs it or not.

0565.
Having a two year old is like using a blender without the lid.

0566.
Every time I'm sad, I just envision a T-Rex trying to put a hat on.

0567.
Burning bridges takes too long. I prefer dynamite.

0568.
Kentucky: Thirteen million people. Fourteen million teeth.

0569.
Cleaning your house with toddlers around is like shoveling snow during a blizzard.

0570.
I hate it when it's dark and my brain says, "You know what we haven't thought about lately? Ghosts and monsters."

0571.
If you're wrong and you shut up, you're wise. If you're right and you shut up, you're married.

0572.
Before you agree to marry someone, ask yourself if they'll be a good zombie killing partner after the apocalypse.

0573.
I hate it when I forget to forward a chain letter and then I die the next day.

0574.
The worst thing about parallel parking is eye witnesses.

0575.
I used to be a people person, but people ruined that for me.

0576.
It was so cold yesterday, I saw a gangsta pull his pants up.

0577.
Everybody wants to be a gangsta until they get punched in the face. Then they want to call the cops.

0578.
We will probably never understand black holes. Or, why women fall totally in love with douche bags.

0579.
You can lead a human to knowledge but you can't make him think.

0580.
The early bird gets the worm, but the second mouse gets the cheese.

0581.
Why should I press "1" for English when you're just going to transfer me to someone who doesn't speak it?

0582.
My computer is frozen up. Maybe it'll work if I click on *everything!*

0583.
Started a new exercise program today, and spent half an hour on the treadmill. I'm so motivated that tomorrow I might even turn it on.

0584.
Where are we going and why am I in this hand basket?

0585.
Don't you hate it when you lose a chip in the salsa, so you send in a recon chip and lose it too?

0586.
Alabama: Seventeen million people. Seventy six last names.

0587.
I'm not random. You just can't think as fast as I can.

0588.
My unicorn died. My dragon flew away. My imaginary friend went on vacation. I'm afraid I'm going sane.

0589.
Has anyone seen my jacket? It's white with a cute belt and long sleeves that make me hug myself.

0590.
Ever had that feeling where you just want to jump right out of bed? Me neither.

0591.
I'm smiling because you've finally all driven me insane.

0592.
The internet is a lot like ancient Egypt. A lot of people write on walls and worship cats.

0593.
I don't think I could complete anybody. But driving someone insane is a definite possibility.

0594.
Last night I went into a bar that was playing music from the 70s. At first, I was afraid, I was petrified.

0595.
Top five things men understand about women:

0596.
My version of a triathlon is a pizza, a burrito supreme and a jelly donut.

0597.
People say everything happens for a reason. So when I punch you in the face and knock you out, remember there was a reason.

0598.
Sometimes I sit and ponder, and I wonder why I'm not in an insane asylum. Then I look at all of you and it occurs to me that maybe I am.

0599.
For Sale: Golden retriever, 1 year old. Tired of waiting for him to retrieve gold. Will consider trade for metal detector.

0600.
In thirty years, the hardest thing our kids will have to do is finding a screen name that isn't already taken.

0601.
I was going to go for a run, and then remembered I don't have a pack of wolves chasing me.

0602.
It's time to pull over and change the air in your head.

0603.
Caution: I overstep my boundaries every ten minutes or so.

0604.
If a lawyer and a politician were both drowning and you could only save one of them, would you go to lunch or read the paper?

0605.
My body is just a filter. Coffee goes in, sarcasm comes out.

0606.
They should put more bacon in each package, so that there's enough for two people.

0607.
If at first you don't succeed, you probably shouldn't try skydiving.

0608.
I think I'm allergic to mornings.

0609.
"Yay, it's Monday again!" said no one ever.

0610.
Sometimes people want to ask deep and thought provoking questions really early in the morning. It's okay to kill those people.

0611.
I'm banned from Walmart until after Christmas. Who knew there was a rule against turning on all the dancing bears in the toy aisle?

0612.
Have you ever looked at someone and just knew that the wheel was still turning but the hamster was dead?

0613.
I hate it when you have to be nice to someone you really want to throw a rock at.

0614.
Everybody wants a smartass know it all for a friend. You're welcome. I'm glad to help.

0615.
My friend told me I could use vodka for housecleaning, and it worked! The more I drank, the cleaner the house looked.

0616.
The world can be really amazing when you're slightly insane.

0617.
I'd offer you moral support, but I have questionable morals.

0618.
I am starting to think I will never be old enough to know better.

0619.
I had a great time last night. Anybody got bail money?

0620.
Balloons are so weird. It's like, "Happy birthday. Here's a round plastic sack of my breath."

0621.
What do you call a fake noodle? An impasta.

0622.
If you pull the wings off a fly, does it become a walk?

0623.
I have lived a long and rewarding life. And not once have I ever had to do algebra in a real world situation.

0624.
Money can't buy you happiness, but it'll rent you a hooker. And for some guys, that's kinda the same thing.

0625.
Forgive your enemies but write down their names and keep the list in a safe place in case they kill you

0626.
If you help a man when he is in need, he'll remember you the next time he's in need.

0627.
Alcohol doesn't solve any problems, but then again milk doesn't either.

0628.
Dancing cheek to cheek is really just a form of floor play.

0629.
The trouble with trouble is that it starts out as fun.

0630.
Bacon is the duct tape of the kitchen. It can fix anything.

0631.
Don't you hate it when you offer someone a sincere compliment on their mustache, and all of a sudden she's not your friend anymore?

0632.
When I die, I want someone to go to my funeral dressed as the grim reaper, and just stand there laughing.

0633.
Teach your kids about taxes. Eat thirty percent of their ice cream.

0634.
A short non-fiction story: My house was clean. Then the kids got up. The end.

0635.
Money can't buy you happiness, but it's more comfortable crying in a Porsche than on a bicycle.

0636.
I had a blast last night. At least that's what it said on the police report.

0637.
I feel bad for kids these days that see a cool toy on TV, but can't have it because their parents have to be over 18 to order it.

0638.
Some people create their own storms and then complain when it rains.

0639.
I heard a loud whining in my car today. I took it to a mechanic and he turned off the Taylor Swift CD.

0640.
I need a whole new perspective on life. Or maybe just ice cream. Yeah, I'll have ice cream.

0641.
Notice: Poor planning on your part does not constitute an emergency on my part.

0642.
Cat puns freak meowt. Seriously, I'm not kitten.

0643.
I'm not clumsy or paranoid. It's just that the chairs, walls and floors all hate me and are out to get me.

0644.
Knowledge is knowing a tomato is a fruit. Wisdom is not putting it into a fruit salad.

0645.
My doctor said I should eat at KFC more often. Actually, he said, "Less McDonald's," but I know what he meant.

0646.
Taking your kids to work is a great way to combine the two most annoying things in your life.

0647.
Without stupid people we would have no one to laugh at. Take the time to thank a stupid person for their contribution.

0648.
Many years of intense therapy has convinced me it's all your fault.

0649.
I am making a list of the biggest mistakes of my life. Just for accuracy purposes, how do you spell your name again?

0650.
You remind me of my Chinese friend, Ug Lee.

0651.
Einstein developed a theory about space. And it was about time too.

0652.
I had a friend once, but the rope broke and he got away.

0653.
I don't know about you guys, but I'm still just a little bit upset that they never did tell us how to get to Sesame Street.

0654.
There are only two ingredients in trail mix: M&Ms and disappointments.

0655.
Women spend more time thinking about what men think than men actually spend thinking.

0656.
Warning: No stupidity beyond this point.

0657.
Don't you hate it when you don't forward that email to seven people within the required seven hours… and you die the next day?

0658.
Ladies, I hate to tell you this but wearing high heels is not sexy if you walk like a newborn calf.

0659.
Being offended does not make you right.

0660.
It never fails to amaze me just how much stupid some people's brains can hold.

0661.
Some people just need a high five. In the face. With a hammer.

0662.
A bicycle cannot stand on its own because it's two tired.

0663.
Who was the marketing genius who called them killer whales? Why didn't they call them sea pandas?

0664.
What's this whole thing about white crayons? Why are they there and what do they want from us?

0665.
If still wearing my pajamas at 5 p.m. is wrong, I don't wanna be right.

0665a.
At my funeral, I'd like there to be a piñata so that people can be happy. But filled with hornets, so they're not too happy.

0667.
If someone throws a rock at you, throw a flower back at them. But remember to throw the vase along with it.

0668.
As a young child my mother told me I could be anyone I wanted to be. Well, it turns out that's called identity theft.

0669.
When I was a kid… oh, wait. I still do that.

0670.
Don't worry. Zombies crave brains. You're safe.

0671.
Never be afraid to try something that's never been done before. Remember, amateurs built the ark. Professionals built the Titanic.

0672.
I don't care how old I am. If I go into a restaurant where they pass out crayons and activity sheets, I want them!

0673.
Wanna know what I got for Christmas? Fat. I got fat for Christmas.

0674.
I have finally figured out the bond that holds my friends and I together… Crazy Glue.

0675.
Are you on Facebook *again?* I mean, *seriously?*

0676.
"See the woman shopping in her pajamas? Isn't she attractive?" Said no one ever.

0677.
Think of a number between 0 and 20. Add 32 to it. Multiply by 2. Now close your eyes… dark, isn't it?

0678.
I couldn't ask for better friends. Maybe some that were more normal. But certainly none better.

0679.
Best feeling ever: Waking up and seeing you have a couple more hours to sleep.

0680.
Don't you hate it when you see a ten year old with a better phone than you?

0681.
I hate it when people don't understand my sarcasm. They ruin everything and should be killed.

0682.
A lie gets halfway around the world before the truth gets its pants on.

0683.
Sometimes even *I'm* afraid of the ideas I come up with.

0684.
Sometimes I forget how to spell a word, so I change a whole sentence just to avoid using it.

0685.
Did you know that a large gathering of baboons is called a "congress?" That explains a lot, doesn't it?

0686.
It's all fun and games until the cops show up. Then it's all hide and go seek.

0687.
Never do anything you wouldn't want to explain to the paramedics.

0688.
Stop congratulating me. I haven't put my other foot on the scale yet.

0689.
What doesn't kill you makes you stronger. Except for bears. Bears will kill you and eat you.

0690.
Yes, I'm weird. You say that like it's a bad thing.

0691.
A jealous woman does better research than the FBI.

0692.
Does running late count as exercise?

0693.
Only two things known to man can change a woman's mood: The words "I love you" and a shoe sale.

0694.
When a woman asks you to guess her age, it's a lot like trying to decide whether to cut the red, blue or green wire.

0695.
I'll call it a "smart" phone the day I yell, "Where's my stupid phone?" and it says, "Over here, under the couch."

0696.
Good friends don't let you do stupid things… alone.

0697.
I wish Noah had just swatted those two mosquitoes.

0698.
Two things: (1) Where have you been my whole life? (2) Can you go back there?

0699.
Alcohol and calculus don't mix. So never drink and derive.

0700.
Of course I'm insane. Life is so much more interesting that way.

0701.
If I'm ever on life support, unplug me and then plug me back in. See if that works.

0702.
I named my dog "five miles" so I can tell my friends I walk five miles every day.

0703.
We are all grownups until somebody pulls out bubble wrap.

0704.
People accuse me all the time of acting the fool. But I'm not acting.

0705.
I don't burn bridges. I just loosen the bolts on them a little each day.

0706.
YOU! Get off my planet!

0707.
I may be schizophrenic, but at least I have each other.

0708.
People text me "PLZ" because it's shorter than "please." I say "NO" because it's shorter than "yes."

0709.
Facebook: Where idiots complain about other idiots being idiots.

0710.
Families are like fudge. Mostly sweet with a few nuts.

0711.
I do yoga to alleviate stress. Just kidding. I get drunk.

0712.
Humanity is losing its geniuses. Aristotle died, Newton died, Einstein died, and I'm not feeling well today.

0713.
I have to step out. If I'm not back in five minutes, just wait longer.

0714.
Relax. We're all crazy. It's not a competition.

0715.
Since I'm old now, I don't fight anymore. Now I just chamber a round. It's easy, I get my point across, and I don't bruise my knuckles anymore.

0716.
It takes a certain kind of person to handle my kinda crazy.

0717.
I dream of a better world, where chickens can cross the road without their motives being questioned.

0718.
Facebook is the only place where it's acceptable to talk to a wall.

0719.
Did you ever just wake up and say, "No way!" and then roll over and go back to sleep?

0720.
I see stupid people. They're everywhere. They walk around like everyone else. They don't even know they're stupid.

0721.
The next time you see someone crying, ask them if it's because of their haircut.

0722.
Please keep calling me crazy, so when they find your body I can plead insanity.

0723.
Dear God, Mosquitoes? Seriously?

0724.
I was thinking of going to Walmart, but I can't find my pajamas.

0725.
I spent half of my money on alcohol, women and gambling. The rest I wasted.

0726.
Last year I asked Santa for the sexiest person ever for Christmas. I woke up in a box.

0727.
Is it wrong to go up to a person with an eye patch and ask, "Was it all fun and games up until that point?"

0728.
My doctor told me he's sorry, but there is no cure for my particular strain of stupid.

0729.
Who needs Google? My wife knows everything.

0730.
Me? Delusional? I should jump down off this unicorn and kick your butt.

0731.
Just let me drink my coffee and no one will get hurt.

0732.
If a zombie apocalypse happened in Las Vegas, would it stay in Las Vegas?

0733.
Whenever I do something right, no one seems to remember. But when I do something wrong, no one seems to forget.

0734.
Some people need a kiss. On the head. From a crocodile.

0735.
If you can't beat them… arrange to have them beaten.

0736.
"The thing about quotes on the internet is that you cannot confirm they are legitimate."   -Abraham Lincoln-

0737.
If I'm guilty of anything, it's that I love too much. And that whole mass murderer thing. But mostly, loving too much.

0738.
I'm unreliable, disorganized, inefficient, unmotivated and immature. But I'm fun.

0739.
Keep it up and you'll be the strange smell in my trunk.

0740.
When the zombie apocalypse finally happens, I'm going straight to the graveyard to play the best game of whack-a-mole ever.

0741.
I just bought $200 worth of groceries. Then I ordered pizza because I was so tired of lugging groceries I didn't want to cook.

0742.
If the best restaurant in your town is attached to a gas station, you probably live in Alabama.

0743.
Cleaning house with kids around is like shoveling the sidewalks during a blizzard.

0744.
A day like coffee is like something without something.

0745.
Don't try to understand women. Women understand women and they hate each other.

0746.
Don't just laugh. Answer the avocado.

0747.
Trying to understand a teenager is like trying to smell the color blue.

0748.
I wonder if clouds ever look down at us and say, "Hey, look. That one looks like a moron."

0749.
Watching TV won't solve your problems. But then, neither will housework.

0750.
It's too bad that stupidity isn't painful.

0751.
Yeah, yeah, world domination. Let me finish my coffee first.

0752.
On the interstate, getting passed by a minivan is the football equivalent of getting tackled by the punter.

0753.
Put the politicians on minimum wage and see how fast things change.

0754.
Someone asked me if I had a date for Valentine's Day. I said, "Yes. February 14th."

0755.
At my age, rolling out of bed is easy… Getting up off the floor is another story.

0756.
I love everybody. Some I love to be around. Some I love to hide from. And some I'd just love to kick in the ankles.

0757.
Some people are so poor, all they have is money.

0758.
When one door closes another door opens. Or, you can just open the closed door. That's how doors work.

0759.
Seen on baby's t-shirt: "Thank you, Mom and Dad, for not naming me North West."

0760.
I wish just once, someone would call me "Sir," without adding, "You're making a scene."

0761.
You say I'm insane like it's a bad thing.

0762.
When a deaf person sees me yawn, do they think I'm screaming?

0763.
I do six sit-ups every morning. That may not sound like much, but there are only so many times you can hit the snooze button.

0764.
My dentist told me I needed a crown. I said, "Yes, I've always thought that."

0765.
I don't go crazy. I am crazy. I just go normal sometimes.

0766.
My imaginary friend and unicorn both think you have serious mental problems.

0767.
The more I hang around people, the more I like dogs.

0768.
Sometimes I question my own sanity. Occasionally it answers me back.

0769.
We should be able to text 911, just in case we're hiding from a killer and can't talk.

0770.
Every time somebody writes ROFL I hear Scooby Doo trying to say waffle.

0771.
People say that I am crazy, cheap and easy. But they're wrong. I'm not cheap.

0772.
When I get a headache I take two aspirin and keep away from children, just like the bottle says.

0773.
When I was your age, we fought with fists. Not cap locks.

0774.
Make yourself at home. Do my dishes.

0775.
Today I wanted to give a shout out to sidewalks, for keeping me off the streets.

0776.
Please stop asking me why I'm still single. I don't ask you how you're still married.

0777.
I already want to take a nap tomorrow.

0778.
Life is too serious to be taken seriously.

0779.
If you're cooler than me, does that mean I'm hotter than you?

0780.
Every time somebody calls me and says "Who is this?" I always answer, "Jake. From State Farm."

0781.
Whoever said the only two things in life were death and taxes forgot laundry and dishes.

0782.
Be happy in front of people you don't like. It drives them crazy.

0783.
I will be posting telepathically today, so if you think of something funny, that was me.

0784.
I was at the ball game yesterday, and I wondered why that baseball was getting bigger and bigger. Then it hit me.

0785.
You may not have lost all your marbles, but there's definitely a hole in the bag.

0786.
I refuse to be a pawn for any man. A woman, maybe. But never a man.

0787.
Warning: I have been left unsupervised today. I am not responsible for what happens.

0788.
During the day, I don't believe in ghosts. At night, I'm a little more open-minded.

0789.
You can't fix stupid. But you can vote it out of office.

0790.
I hate it when Wikipedia copies my entire homework assignment.

0791.
I am not a minion of evil. I am upper management.

0792.
Is everything really that expensive, or am I just poor?

0793.
Drink espresso. Do more stupid things faster.

0794.
In my generation, zombies didn't run. They walked. Uphill. In the snow. And they finished all the brains on their plates, and they liked it.

0795.
Vegetarian *(noun)*: Old Indian word for lousy hunter.

0796.
Let's all celebrate Columbus Day by walking into someone else's house and telling them we live there now.

0797.
"Awesome" ends with "me." Coincidence? Hardly.

0798.
I'm not stalking you. I'm doing intense research.

0799.
The last thing I want to do is hurt you. But it's still on the list.

0800.
My GPS has learned to say, "No, stupid. Your other left."

0801.
Three out of the four voices in my head want to sleep. The other one wants to know if bees really do have knees.

0802.
Coffee makes your brain go, "Wheeeeee!"

0803.
Some days, the best thing about my job is that my chair spins.

0804.
I asked one hundred women what shampoo they used in the shower. The number one response was, "Who are you and how did you get in my house?"

0805.
I may be old, but I got to see all the cool bands.

0806.
The reason kids have so much energy is because they siphon it out of their parents like midget gas thieves.

0807.
While you were judging others, you left your closet door open and all your skeletons fell out.

0808.
Things to do today: (1) Dig a big hole. (2) Name it love (3) Watch people falling in love

0809.
Enjoy life. There's plenty of time to be dead.

0810.
There appears to be a strange new trend at my office. People are naming the food in the office refrigerator. Today I ate a sandwich named Kevin.

0811.
Dear Tequila, We had a deal. You were supposed to make me funnier, better looking, and a great dancer. I saw the video. We need to talk.

0812.
Cartoons and prison: The only two places where you can wear the same thing every day and nobody cares.

0813.
Best friend: *(noun):* Someone who knows how crazy you are and chooses to hang around you anyway.

0814.
Chaos, panic, disorder and mayhem. Good, my work here is done.

0815.
I'm a multi-tasking procrastinator. I can put off all kinds of things at once.

0816.
I thought I was wrong once, but I was mistaken.

0817.
A friend will calm you down when you're angry. A best friend will walk beside you, carrying a bat, saying, "Somebody's gonna get it."

0818.
Today is the first day of the rest of your life. But then again, so was yesterday and look how badly you screwed that up.

0819.
Redneck divorce: "Get outa the truck."

0820.
Don't mess with old guys. They can't fight you anymore, so they'll just kill you instead. Then they'll take a nap.

0821.
If a man speaks in the forest and there is no woman to hear him, is he still wrong?

0822.
When I die, I want my last words to be, "I left a million dollars under the…"

0823.
Patience is what you have when there are too many witnesses around.

0824.
Of course you can trust the government. Just ask an Indian.

0825.
You know you just won the argument when your adversary responds with, "Whatever."

0826.
For your information, I did not escape. They gave me a day pass.

0827.
My New Year's resolution was to lose thirty pounds by the end of summer. I only have forty pounds to go.

0828.
I just took a shower. You have no idea how difficult it was sneaking that thing out of Home Depot.

0829.
Be yourself. Everyone else is taken.

0830.
Life is a playground. Get out and play.

0831.
When she says "I'm only going to one store, please come with me." Don't go! It's a trap!

0832.
My bed is a magical place where I suddenly remember everything I was supposed to do.

0833.
Mephobia: *(noun):* Fear of becoming so awesome that the rest of the world can't handle it and everybody dies.

0834.
If you love someone, let them go. If they come back, nobody else wanted them either.

0835.
The problem with political jokes is they get elected.

0836.
If only closed minds came with closed mouths.

0837.
Santa saw your Facebook photos. You're getting clothes and a dictionary for Christmas.

0838.
Well, aren't you just a fun filled little gumdrop double dipped in psycho?

0839.
I don't care how old I am, I still like cartoons.

0840.
There is a time and a place for decaf coffee. Never, and in the trash.

0841.
Did you hear about the dyslexic Satanist? He sold his soul to Santa.

0842.
They say you are what you eat. That's funny. I don't remember eating a sexy beast this morning.

0843.
My neighbor knocked on my door at 3 a.m. this morning. Can you imagine that? 3 a.m.! Luckily, I was still up playing my drums.

0844.
Sorry my house is messy. It was clean yesterday. You should have come then.

0845.
My dad used to swear and then say, "Pardon my French." Today in class the teacher asked us if anyone knew any French. I raised my hand…

0846.
Behind every great man is a woman, rolling her eyes and shaking her head.

0847.
Oh, so you're eleven years old and have an iPad. Good for you. When I was eleven, I had an *imagination.*

0848.
When life gives you lemons, give them grapefruit juice. Then sit back and laugh as they try to figure out how you did it.

0849.
My grandpa's advice: Keep all skunks and bankers at a safe distance.

0850.
My grandpa's advice: Life is simpler when you plow around the stump.

0851.
My grandpa's advice: A hornet is considerably faster than a John Deere tractor.

0852.
My grandpa's advice: Forgive your enemies. It messes with their heads.

0853.
My grandpa's advice: When you wallow with pigs, expect to get dirty.

0854.
My grandpa's advice: Timing has a lot to do with the outcome of a rain dance.

0855.
My grandpa's advice: Sometimes you get, and sometimes you get got.

0856.
If you start thinking of yourself as somebody with some influence, try ordering somebody else's dog around.

0857.
So, I needed help with a word for a crossword puzzle I was working on, and I called a friend. He hung up on me. Can you believe that? People sure are cranky at 3 a.m.

0858.
I've noticed that the squirrels are starting to gather nuts for the winter. I thought I'd better check on you to make sure you have a safe place to hide.

0859.
Want to freak out your neighbors? Rename your WiFi "NSA Surveillance Van"

0860.
You can't buy happiness. But you can buy tequila, and that's kinda the same thing.

0861.
People ask me why I swear. I swear because sometimes "darnit" and "meanie head" just don't cover it.

0862.
Diapers and politicians should be changed often and for the same reason.

0863.
Raisin cookies that look like chocolate chip cookies are the reason I have trust issues.

0864.
I love alcohol because no great story ever started with someone eating a salad.

0865.
I just stepped on a tack. And no, I didn't cry like a baby. Babies do not have the lung capacity or the vocabulary to do what I just did.

0866.
When people tell me "You're gonna regret that in the morning," I sleep until noon. Because hey, I'm a problem solver.

0867.
I stopped believing for a few minutes this morning. Journey is gonna be so mad at me when they find out.

0868.
Sometimes my only success for the day is getting the laundry in the dryer before it starts to mildew.

0869.
The difference between pizza and your opinion is that I asked for pizza.

0870.
Need a friend? Call me. Need a laugh? Call me. Need to borrow money? This number has been disconnected.

0871.
Don't take life so seriously. You won't get out of it alive.

0872.
Remember, when you die, you can't take it with you. But you can let me hold it until you come back.

0873.
The Beatles: Better than Bieber since 1961.

0874.
I just got off the phone with my mom. She had a nice talk.

0875.
Jehovah's Witnesses don't celebrate Halloween. Apparently they don't like it when random people show up at their door.

0876.
All you need is love. But a little ice cream now and then doesn't hurt.

0877.
Single *(noun)*: A man who jokes about women in the kitchen.

0878.
When you stop believing in Santa, you get underwear.

0879.
Having plans sounds like a good idea in theory, but then you have to put on clothes and leave your house.

0880.
I live in a tiny madhouse ruled by a tiny army of sadists that I made myself.

0881.
Of all the possible utensils they could have chosen to eat rice with, how did two sticks win?

0882.
When you are dead, you do not know you are dead. It is only difficult and sad for those around you. It is the same when you are stupid.

0883.
They told me I could be anything I wanted. So I became everything.

0884.
I joined the Hokey Pokey Rehabilitation Center. So I could turn myself around.

0885.
So, when is this "old enough to know better" supposed to kick in?

0886.
I love it when I buy a bag of air and they're nice enough to throw in two or three potato chips.

0887.
The psychic fair has been cancelled for tomorrow, due to unforeseen circumstances.

0888.
I wouldn't kill so many houseplants if they could scream for food and water like children do.

0889.
Be nice to your kids. They'll be choosing your nursing home.

0890.
I'm not as random as you think I salad.

0891.
Age is not important unless you are a cheese or a bottle of wine.

0892.
Fact: The average body has just enough bones to make an entire human skeleton.

0893.
Do not judge me. I was born to be awesome, not perfect.

0894.
I don't know if it's the same for everybody else, but I've thought about running away more as an adult than a child.

0895.
I want to sleep but my brain won't stop talking to itself.

0896.
There are only 10 types of people in this world. Those who understand binary and those who don't.

0897.
Two mysterious people live in my house. Somebody and nobody. Somebody did it and nobody knows who.

0898.
Don't judge me. If you're reading this, then you don't have a job either.

0899.
I entered ten puns in a contest to see which one would win. No pun in ten did.

0900.
Good moms let you lick the beaters. Great moms turn them off first.

0901.
Outside of a dog, a book is man's best friend. Inside of a dog, it's too dark to read.

0902.
My wife asked me what I was going to do today. I said, Nothing." She said, "Didn't you do that yesterday?" I said, "I wasn't finished."

0903.
Remember when we were young, and couldn't wait to grow up? Were we stupid, or what?

0904.
Yawning is just your body's way of telling you that you only have 20 % of battery remaining.

0905.
I seldom brag, but my son is inmate of the month at Victorville State Prison.

0906.
If life gives you lemons, KEEP THEM! Because, hey, free lemons!

0907.
HAPPY BIRTHDAY! (One in 365 people will be freaked out by this)

0908.
Insanity does not run in my family. It strolls through at a leisurely pace and takes the time to get close to everyone.

0909.
I'm lost. I've gone to look for myself. If I should return before I get back, please ask me to wait.

0910.
I was always taught to respect my elders, but it's getting harder and harder to find one.

0911.
I've always been crazy, but it's kept me from going insane.

0912.
Buying Halloween candy early means you'll be buying Halloween candy twice.

0913.
Dear Karma, I have a list of people you've missed.

0914.
Beautify Texas. Put a yankee on a bus.

0915.
A book screams and commits suicide every time you watch Jersey Shore.

0916.
Normal people scare me. But nowhere near as much as I scare them.

0917.
ABRACADABRA!   Oh, rats! You're still here!

0918.
Do you know what the difference is between a lawyer and an onion? You cry when you cut up an onion.

0919.
I'm known around the world for my tendency to exaggerate.

0920.
I tend to offend everyone occasionally. If I haven't offended you yet, please take a number and wait.

0921.
Last words of a redneck: "Here, hold my beer."

0922.
For men who think a woman's place is in the kitchen, remember that's where the knives are kept.

0923.
I can't believe the cop put me in the back seat when I clearly called shotgun.

0924.
There are only 10 types of people in this world. Those who understand binary and those who don't.

0925.
Be nice to your kids. They'll be choosing your nursing home.

0926.
I'm almost always late for work. But I leave early to make up for it.

0927.
Sometimes I think the world has gone completely mad. And then I think, "Oh, who cares?" and then I think, "I want a sandwich."

0928.
When people tell me "You're gonna regret that in the morning," I sleep until noon. Because hey, I'm a problem solver.

0929.
Dijon vu: the same mustard as before.

0930.
You can't scare me. I have children.

0931.
Help! I've fallen and I… hey, nice carpet!

0932.
I'm telling you, officer, he was dead when I got here!

0933.
A shotgun wedding I a case of wife or death.

0934.
Oh, I'm sorry. Did my back hurt your knife?

0935.
Don't be so serious. If you can't laugh at yourself, call me. I'll be happy to laugh at you.

0936.
A man needs a mistress just to break the monogamy.

0937.
When I die I'm gonna come back and haunt all you guys.

0938.
A hangover is the wrath of grapes.

0939.
Does the name Pavlov ring a bell?

0940.
Sarcasm: *(noun):* The brain's natural defense against the less intelligent.

0941.
Condoms should be used on every conceivable occasion.

0942.
Follow your heart. But take your brain with you.

0943.
I've been ignored by much better people than you.

0944.
Time flies like an arrow. Fruit flies like a banana.

0945.
I have CDO. It's like OCD but all the letters are in alphabetical order like they should be.

0946.
When she got married, she got a new name and a dress.

0947.
When your parents accuse you of lying, look them right in the eye and yell, Easter Bunny! Santa Claus! Tooth Fairy!"

0948.
I'm not arguing. I'm merely explaining why I'm right.

0949.
Smile. It'll either warm their heart or piss them off. Either way, you win.

0950.
A midget fortune teller who escapes from prison is a small medium at large.

0951.
Once you've seen one shopping center, you've seen a mall.

0952.
Bakers trade bread secrets on a knead-to-know basis

0953.
I live my life by only two rules. (1) If it makes me happy, I do it. (2) If it doesn't, I don't.

0954.
Santa's helpers are subordinate clauses

0955.
My cousin Cletus says a possum is a flat animal that sleeps in the middle of the road.

0956.
Acupuncture is a jab well done.

0957.
There are 5,000 different kinds of spiders, and at least 4,800 of them live in my house.

0958.
My child sold your "honor student" the answers to the test.

0959.
In Texas, "fixinto" is a real word.

0960.
In Alabama, the first day of deer season is a state holiday. Seriously.

0961.
Being kind is more important than being right.

0962.
I'm fine. The rest of you need therapy.

0963.
Time wounds all heels.

0964.
What do you throw to a drowning lawyer? His partners.

0965.
No matter how serious your life requires you to be, we all need a friend we can be goofy with.

0966.
Opportunities are never lost. Someone will take the ones you miss.

0967.
I'm sorry, did you say something? I couldn't hear you over the roar of my awesomeness.

0968.
I didn't get the job. They asked me what my greatest achievement was at my last job. All my Farmville stuff failed to impress them.

0969.
Don't try to figure me out. I'm a special kind of twisted.

0970.
I'm not the black sheep of the family. I'm the whole flock.

0971.
It's always better to let people consider you a fool, than to speak and remove all doubt.

0972.
It's unfair. A baby drinks a bottle and falls asleep and it's okay. But when I drink a bottle and fall asleep everyone calls me an alcoholic. Where's the justice?

0973.
Come on, now, honey. Just lower your standards a little. I did.

0974.
There is a black sheep in every family. Look closely at your relatives. If they appear normal, it's you.

0975.
I found out the hard way that sarcasm just doesn't work in a text message.

0976.
What do you have if three lawyers are buried up to their necks in concrete?   Not enough cement.

0977.
Common sense is so rare these days it should be considered a super power.

0978.
I don't know karate, but I do know crazy. And I'm not afraid to use it.

0979.
Lately, my whole attitude on life has changed. I've gone from, "Maybe I shouldn't do this…" to "What the hell, let's see what happens."

0980.
Dear Media, Please stop making stupid people famous for no reason. Thank you.

0981.
A relationship with no trust is like a cell phone with no service provider. Your only option is to play games.

0982.
Dear Life, when I asked you if my day could possibly get any worse, I meant it as a rhetorical question.

0983.
I would have loved to have been there when the guy who discovered milk had to explain how.

0984.
I put my new cell phone on airplane mode and threw it in the air. It didn't fly. I feel ripped off.

0985.
Rhinos are nothing more than fat unicorns.

0986.
I was going to clean my room, but then I turned on music and went into dance mode.

0987.
I keep my house messy on purpose so that if someone breaks in and tries to kill me, they'll trip over something. It's a safety measure.

0988.
Everyone is entitled to their opinion. Except people who don't like bacon.

0989.
If you don't want a sarcastic answer, don't ask a stupid question.

0990.
Don't you hate it when you're in a quiet room full of people and you're eating something really crunchy?

0991.
I don't like to brag, but I once made it to the third level in Donkey Kong.

0992.
I don't misspell words. I invent new ones.

0993.
I work very well with others. As long as they leave me the hell alone.

0994.
The rate at which sarcasm is released from my mouth is directly proportional to the rate at which stupidity is released from yours.

0995.
Never underestimate the stupidity of idiots.

0996.
I've never been guilty of road rage. But I certainly understand it.

0997.
When all the dust settles, aren't we all just looking for that one right person? Someone who knows which songs not to talk over?

0998.
Do not read the next sentence! You little rebel. I like you. We're gonna get along great.

0999.
I am offended that you don't find me as funny as I find me.

1000.
I've started singing in the shower. It drowns out the sound of the kids beating on the bathroom door.

1001.
When someone tells you nothing is impossible, tell him to dribble a barbell.

*****

We know, we know… we only promised you 1,001 statuses. But a few of them were real stinkers, so here's some more to make up for it…

*****

1002.
The brain is the hardest working organ in the human body. It works for you 24 hours a day, seven days a week, from the day you are born until the day you fall in love.

1003.
Conclusion *(noun):* The point at which you got tired of thinking.

1004.
Whether or not you support the right to bear arms depends on which end of the gun you're on.

1005.
If you're competing for bitch of the year, I think it's safe to say you're winning.

1006.
You're not stupid. You just have bad luck when you think.

1007.
It's not that we grow more patient as we age. It's just that we finally get to the point where we no longer worry about stupid drama.

1008.
Just because you see the bear's teeth doesn't mean he's smiling at you. Women work the same way.

1009.
Her constant nagging just means that she cares. It's not until she goes silent that she's plotting your murder.

1010.
Life is like an elevator. Sometimes on your way to the top, you have to stop and let some people off.

1011.
I don't have a temper problem. I just have a low tolerance for your particular form of stupid.

1012.
It's just a matter of time before they add the word "Syndrome" after my last name.

1013.
I just read that 458,317 people got married last year. Now, I don't want to be picky or anything. But shouldn't that be an even number?

1014.
Of course I support the right to bear arms. Otherwise how would they catch their fish?

1015.
Girls, makeup is expensive. Just buy him beer, and you'll get the same end result.

1016.
I never repeat gossip, so listen closely the first time.

1017.
Thirty isn't old. Unless you're a dog. Or a gallon of milk.

1018.
Warning: My mind has chewed through its leash and is on the loose again.

1019.
The best ten years of a woman's life is between 39 and 40.

1020.
The great thing about old age is you finally know everything. You just can't remember any of it.

1021.
I've already broken all the rules today, so you'll have to make new ones.

1022.
When I die, I want to be buried with some random animal bone just to confuse future archaeologists.

1023.
People like you are the reason why people like me need medication.

1024.
I've got two tickets on the crazy train. Who wants one?

1025.
When you get older the first thing to go is your memory. I can't remember the next thing.

1026.
The first five days after the weekend are always the hardest.

1027.
I can explain it to you. But I can't *understand* it for you.

1028.
Alcoholic *(noun):* Someone you don't like who drinks just as much as you do.

1029.
I am not old. I'm a recycled teenager.

1030.
Over the hill? What hill? I don't remember any hill.

1031.
If you have an opinion about my business, please raise your hand. Now put it over your mouth. Thank you.

1032.
I don't drink to forget. I drink to remember what I ever saw in you.

1033.
Back in my day, we wrote "ha ha," not "LOL"

1034.
First, learn the rules. Then break them.

1035.
I don't drink to get drunk. I drink to stay drunk.

1036.
My head says I need to get up and go to work. But my pillow says I need more sleep.

1037.
There are only two types of honest people in the world. Old drunks and small children.

1038.
John Wayne once said never trust a man that doesn't drink. That's enough of an endorsement for me.

1039.
I'm guess that whoever decided to call it "common sense" didn't know that many people.

1040.
I'm older than the internet. I'll bet you are too.

1041.
Money can't buy happiness, but it can buy bacon. And that's even better.

1042.
Does anyone have any plans to stare at their phone somewhere exciting this weekend?

1043.
At my age, I've seen it all, heard it all and done it all. I just can't remember it all.

1044.
I only have a problem with alcohol when it's all gone

1045.
Time may be the best healer, but it's a really crummy beautician.

1046.
Just because you are talking doesn't mean you're making sense.

1047.
The best way to avoid a hangover is to never stop drinking.

1048.
If I have offended anyone, then my efforts have been rewarded.

1049.
Very few women admit their age. Very few men act theirs.

1050.
You know you're old when you've run out of things to learn the hard way.

1051.
You couldn't handle me even if I came with instructions.

1052.
Is growing up reversible, in case I decide I don't like it?

1053.
Shut up, voices! Or I'll poke you with a Q-Tip again!

1054.
Poor *(Adjective):* When you have too much month left at the end of your money.

1055.
You're never too old to start new bad habits.

1056.
I want that job where you get to push scared skydivers out of airplanes.

1057.
Honk if you love Jesus. Text while driving if you want to meet him.

*****

Thank you for reading
1001 Funny and Witty Twitter Tweets.
We sincerely hope you enjoyed it.

Please enjoy the following
preview of
1001 Funny Jokes You Can Tell Anywhere,
Now available on Amazon.com

*****

112.

A cop pulled over a driver and informed him that because he was wearing his seatbelt, he had just won a thousand dollars in a safety promotion.

"What are you going to do with the money?" the cop asked him.

He said "I guess I'll go to driving school and get my driver's license."

His wife spoke up from the passenger seat. "Don't listen to him, officer. He always turns into a smart aleck when he's drunk."

Their conversation woke up a guy in the back seat who said "I knew we wouldn't get very far in this stolen car."

And just when the cop thought he'd finally heard it all, there was a knock from the trunk and a voice asked "Are we over the border yet?"

113.
You might be a redneck if you come back from the dump with more than you took.

114.
You might be a redneck if you keep a can of raid on the kitchen table.

115.
I went to a book store and asked the salesman "Where's the self-help section?"
He said if he told me, it would defeat the purpose.

116.
   A father saw his teenage son in the back yard, washing the tire swing that hung from an old oak tree. After it was nice and clean, he covered it with car wax and started polishing it to a nice shine.
   Curious, the father went outside and said "Hey, Timmy. I thought you were going golfing with your friends this afternoon."
   "I did," Timmy said. "But the golf instructor told me I needed to work on my swing. So I left."

117.
Johnny: Doc, every time I drink a cup of coffee I get a sharp stabbing pain in my eye. What should I do?
Doctor: Try taking the spoon out of your coffee cup before you drink it.

118.

You might be a redneck if a tornado hits your town and does ten million dollars worth of home improvements.

119.

An old woman is riding in an elevator in a very lavish New York City building when a young, beautiful woman gets into the elevator, smelling of expensive perfume. She turns to the old woman and says arrogantly, "Tittilation" by Ralph Lauren, $150 an ounce!" Then another young and beautiful woman gets on the elevator, and also very arrogantly turns to the old woman saying, "Chanel No. 5, $200 an ounce!" About three floors later, the old woman has reached her destination and is about to get off the elevator. Before she leaves, she looks both beautiful women in the eye, then bends over and farts and says, "Cabbage – 49 cents a head!"

120.

You might be a redneck if you've ever bathed with Lava soap

121.

If you live to be 100, and do one of those interviews with the television station, make up something good. Just to mess with people. Tell them you lived to be a hundred because you ate a pine cone every day, or dabbed your face with mayonnaise every night before you went to bed.

122.
Treat your mom to a margarita next mother's day. Remember, you're the reason she drinks.

123.
Mother was out shopping, and dad was in charge. Their little angel was two years old. Someone had given her a little 'tea set' as a gift, and it was one of her favorite toys. Dad was in the living room engrossed in the evening news when she brought him a little cup of 'tea', which was just water. After several cups of tea and lots of praise for such yummy tea, mom came home. Dad made her wait in the living room to watch her bring him a cup of tea, because it was "just the sweetest thing!" Mom waited, and sure enough, here she came down the hall with a cup of tea for Daddy, and she watched him drink it up. Then she said, to the father, "'Did it ever occur to you that the only place she can reach to get water is the toilet?"

124.
A fun way to waste a couple of hours:
Take some yellow sticky notes and write "Sorry about the damage" on them.
Then put them on random cars in a mall parking lot.
Sit back, relax, and watch the car owners look for the damage.

125.
Q: If a blonde and a brunette jump out of a plane at the same time, who will hit the ground first?
A: The brunette. The blonde will have to stop and ask for directions.

126.
Real testimony in a court of law:
   Q: What gear were you in at the moment of impact?
   A: Adidas sweats and Nike shoes.

127.
A man wrote a letter to a small hotel in a Midwest town he planned to visit on his vacation. He wrote, "I would very much like to bring my dog with me. He is well-groomed and very well behaved. Would you be willing to permit me to keep him in my room with me at night?" An immediate reply came from the hotel owner, who wrote, "Dear sir, I've been operating this hotel for many years. In all that time, I've never had a dog steal towels, bedclothes, silverware or pictures off the walls. I've never had to evict a dog in the middle of the night for being drunk and disorderly. And I've never had a dog run out on a hotel bill. Yes, indeed, your dog is welcome at my hotel. And, if your dog will vouch for you, you're welcome to stay here, too."

128.
If Plan A fails, remember that you have twenty five letters left.

129.
Mary: I went riding yesterday and had trouble with my
       horse. I wanted to go in one direction, and he wanted
       to go in another.
Sue: So, how did you decide?
Mary: He tossed me for it.

130.
You can't buy happiness, but you can buy ice cream. And that's kind of the same thing.

131.
Real testimony in a court of law:
   Q: What day were you born?
   A: May tenth.
   Q: What year?
   A: Every year.

132.
A woman awakes during the night to find that her husband is not in their bed. She puts on her robe and goes down stairs to look for him. She finds him sitting at the kitchen table with a cup of coffee in front him. He appears deep in thought, just staring at the wall. She watches as he wipes a tear from his eye and takes a sip of coffee. "What's the matter, dear?" she whispers as she steps into the room. "Why are you down here at this time of night?" The husband looks up, "Do you remember twenty years ago when we were dating, and you were only 16?" he asks solemnly. "Yes, I do," she replies. The husband pauses. The words are not coming easily. "Do you remember when your father caught us in the back seat of my convertible?" "Yes, I remember," says the wife, sitting into a chair beside him. The husband continues. "Do you remember when he shoved a shotgun in my face and said, "Either you marry my daughter, or I will send you to jail for twenty years". "I remember that too," she replies softly. He wipes another tear from his cheek and says… "I would have gotten out today!"

133.
Did you hear about the two silkworms who had a race? They ended up in a tie.

134.
Real testimony in a court of law:
- Q: What was the first thing your husband said to you that morning?
- A: Good morning Debbie.
- Q: And why did that upset you?
- A: My name is Sally.

135.
Real testimony in a court of law:
- Q: Did you blow your horn?
- A: Before or after the accident?
- Q: Before the accident.
- A: Yes, I played trumpet in the city symphony.

136.
"The car won't start," said a wife to her husband. "I think there's water in the gasoline." "How do you know?" said the husband scornfully. "You don't know anything about cars." "I'm telling you," repeated the wife, "I'm sure there's water in the gasoline." "We'll see," mocked the husband. "Let me check it out. Where's the car?" "At the bottom of the swimming pool."

137.

I was sitting at the bar staring at my drink when a large, tattooed biker steps up next to me, grabs my drink and gulps it down in one swig. "Well, whatcha' gonna do about it?" he says, with his fist in my face. As I burst into tears the biker says, "Come on, man," "I didn't think you'd cry, dude I was just messing with you" "This is the worst day of my life," I said. Everything has gone wrong, I was late to a meeting and my boss fired me. When I went to the parking lot, I found my car had been stolen and I don't have any insurance. I left my wallet in the cab I took home. I found my wife with another man… and then my dog bit me. So I came to this bar to work up the courage to put an end to it all, I buy a drink, I drop a cyanide capsule in and sit here watching the poison dissolve; and then you show up and drink the whole thing! But heck, enough about me. How are you doing?"

138.

Q: What's the difference between God and an attorney?
A: God doesn't think he's an attorney.

139.

Joe goes into a pet store and says "I want to buy a bird."

The clerk says "I have just the bird for you. He's a parrot named Pete. He can sing the Star Spangled Banner and say hello in eight different languages."

Joe says "Never mind all that. Is he tender?"

140.
Real testimony in a court of law:

Q: Have you or your husband ever practiced the occult?

A: Yes, voodoo.

Q: Voodoo?

A: We do.

Q: You do?

A: Yes, voodoo.

141.

The brash captain of a navy battleship saw a bright light in the distance, on a collision course with his ship.

"Radioman, tell that fool to turn starboard twenty degrees and get out of our way."

Aye aye, captain.

A minute later the radioman said "Captain, he refused. He said we need to adjust our course twenty degrees to port."

The brash captain shouted. "Tell him he is talking to a U.S. Navy battleship. We don't change our course for anybody. Find out who that idiot is."

A few moments went by before the radioman spoke again.

"Captain, he says he is the lighthouse at Barber's Point. He suggests you put your life preserver on."

Printed in Great Britain
by Amazon